THEORY OF MUSIC MADE EASY

GRADE 4

Lina Ng

© RHYTHM MP SDN. BHD.1991

Published By
RHYTHM MP SDN. BHD.
1947, Lorong IKS Bukit Minyak 2,
Taman IKS Bukit Minyak, 14100 Simpang Ampat,
Penang, Malaysia.
Tel: +60 4 5050246 (Direct Line), +60 4 5073690 (Hunting Line)
Fax: +60 4 5050691
E-mail: rhythmmp@mphsb.com
Website: www.rhythmmp.com

ISBN 967-985-296-2
Order No.: MPT-3003-04

CONTENTS

Time Signatures

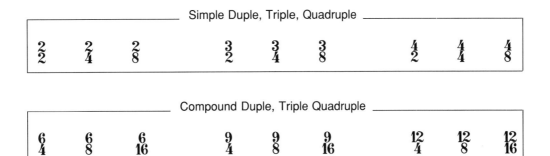

Simple Duple, Triple, Quadruple

Compound Duple, Triple Quadruple

1. Insert the missing figure in the time signature.

(a)

(b)

(c)

(d)

(e)

(f)

(g)

(h)

(i)

(j)

2. Rewrite the rhythm using the new time signature.

(a)

(b)

3. Add bar-lines to the following.

4. Rewrite, using the given time signature.

5. Insert the time signature.

6. Rewrite, adding bar-lines and grouping the notes correctly.

The **C Clef** is printed 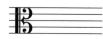, but it can be written ,  or 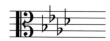.

When the clef is centred on the 3rd line of the stave, it is known as the **Alto Clef**.

The line on which the sign is centred is *middle C.*

The **Alto Clef** is used mainly by the *viola*.

Key signatures are written thus:

---

1. **Name the notes below.**

E   G   B   D

---

2. **Write the tonic triads with key signatures.**

(a)
G major

(e)
D major

(i)
A major

(b)
F major

(f)
E♭ major

(j)
A♭ major

(c)
E minor

(g)
B minor

(k)
C♯ minor

(d)
G minor

(h)
C minor

(l)
F minor

3. Rewrite the passages using the Alto Clef.

Mozart, Sonata 1

(a)

Haydn, Allegro

(b) etc.

Beethoven, Rondo Op.51 No.1

(c)

4. Rewrite the passages using the given clefs.

Haydn, String Quartet in F major Op.24

(a) etc.

Beethoven, Symphony No.1 in C major Op.21

(b)

• •

To add another sharp (♯) to a note which is already sharpened - use a double sharp (𝄪).

A double sharp (𝄪) raises a note 2 semitones.

To add another flat (♭) to a note which is already flattened - use a double flat (♭♭).

A double flat (♭♭) lowers a note 2 semitones.

Example: 'C 𝄪' sounds the same as 'D'

'F 𝄪' sounds the same as 'G'

'E♭♭' sounds the same as 'D'

'B♭♭' sounds the same as 'A'

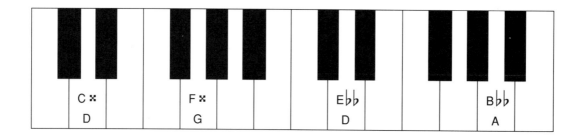

1. First, name the note (e.g. B double flat), then write a note which sounds the same.

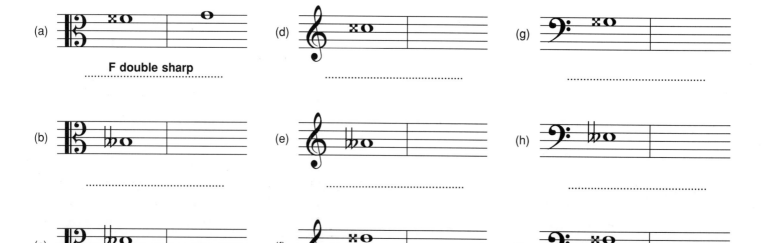

(a)   **F double sharp**

2. After each note, write two other notes (one above, one below) which sound the same.
These notes are enharmonic equivalents of the given note.

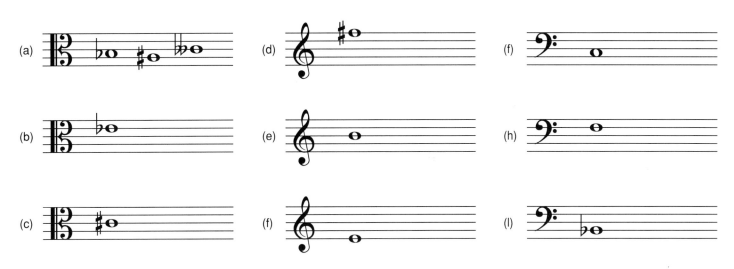

(a) (d) (f)

(b) (e) (h)

(c) (f) (l)

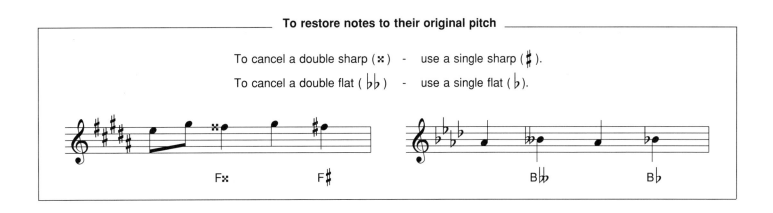

___ **To restore notes to their original pitch** ___

To cancel a double sharp (✗) - use a single sharp (♯).

To cancel a double flat (♭♭) - use a single flat (♭).

F✗   F♯   B♭♭   B♭

3. Restore the notes marked * to their original pitch.

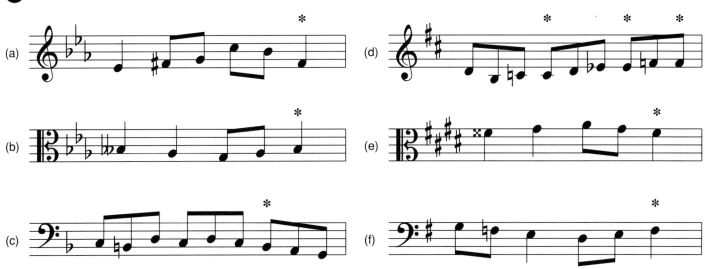

(a) (d)

(b) (e)

(c) (f)

Grade 4

BREVE  = 2 ○

A breve is equals to 2 semibreves.

In $\frac{4}{2}$ time, a silent bar is shown by *a breve rest*.

In all other time signatures, a silent bar is shown by *a bar rest*.

1. Rewrite the scales, doubling the time values.

2. Rewrite the scales, halving the time values.

DOUBLE DOTS - A second dot after a note adds half the length already added by the first dot.

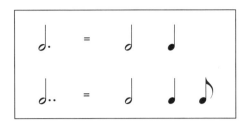

3. Complete the following.

(a) 𝅗𝅥. =

𝅗𝅥.. =

(b) ♪. =

♪.. =

(c) 𝅝· =

𝅝·· =

4. Insert bar-lines to the following.

Grade 4

DUPLETS - A duplet is usually shown by a figure 2 above the notes.

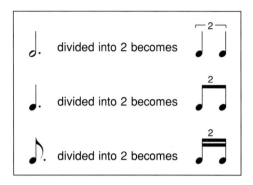

Duplets may also be written as dotted notes.

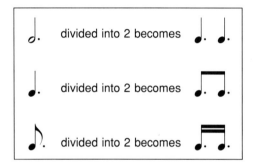

5. **Add bar-lines to the following.**

6. Rewrite the following using the given time signatures.

(a)

(b)

(c)

(d)

(e)
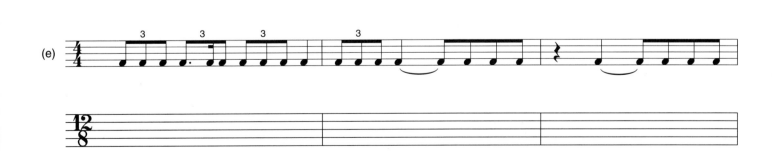

MAJOR KEY	KEY SIGNATURES	MINOR KEY
5 ⎡ G 5 ⎢ D 5 ⎢ A 5 ⎢ E 5 ⎣ B	F♯ F♯ C♯ F♯ C♯ G♯ F♯ C♯ G♯ D♯ F♯ C♯ G♯ D♯ A♯ 5 5 5 5 (Note that they are a 5th apart)	E B F♯ C♯ G♯
4 ⎡ F 4 ⎢ B♭ 4 ⎢ E♭ 4 ⎢ A♭ 4 ⎣ D♭	B♭ B♭ E♭ B♭ E♭ A♭ B♭ E♭ A♭ D♭ B♭ E♭ A♭ D♭ G♭ 4 4 4 4 (Note that they are a 4th apart)	D G C F B♭

The key signature of a Minor Key is the *same* as its Relative Major.
To find its relative major, go up 3 semitones. If it is a black key, treat it as a flat (♭).

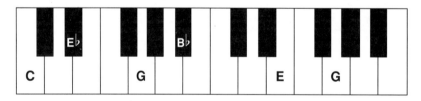

[C minor - E♭ major]   [G minor - B♭ major]   [E minor - G major]

1. Copy the key signatures.

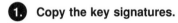

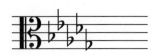

2. Write the tonic triads with key signatures.

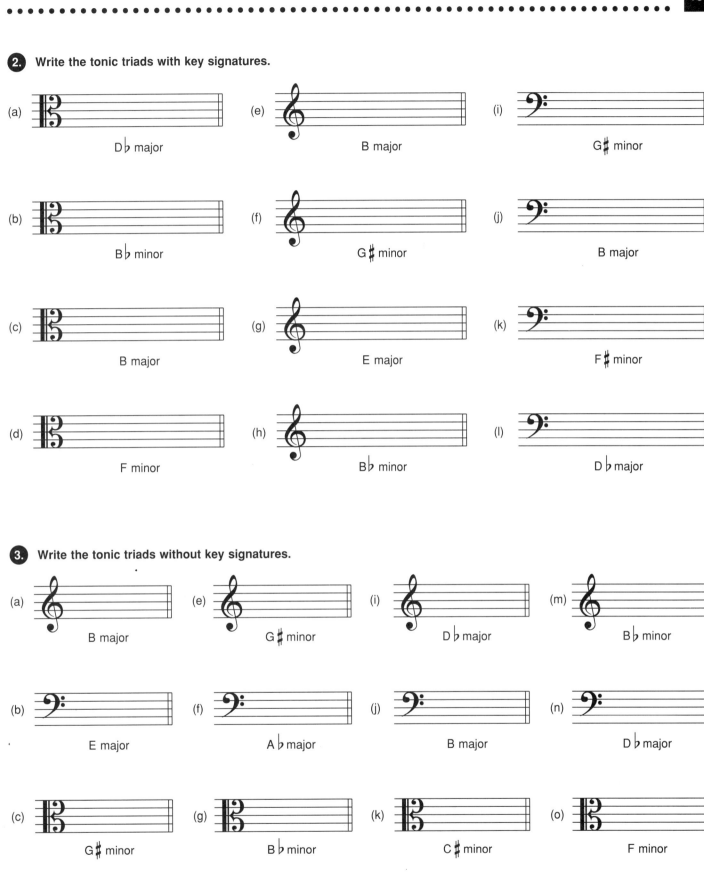

(a) Db major

(b) Bb minor

(c) B major

(d) F minor

(e) B major

(f) G# minor

(g) E major

(h) Bb minor

(i) G# minor

(j) B major

(k) F# minor

(l) Db major

3. Write the tonic triads without key signatures.

(a) B major

(b) E major

(c) G# minor

(d) Db major

(e) G# minor

(f) Ab major

(g) Bb minor

(h) D major

(i) Db major

(j) B major

(k) C# minor

(l) Bb major

(m) Bb minor

(n) Db major

(o) F minor

(p) B major

4. First, name the keys (G♯ harmonic minor, B♭ melodic minor, etc.). Then, mark semitones with ⬚ .

(a)
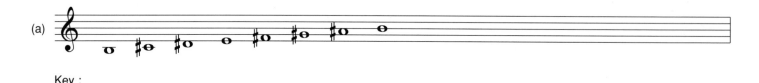

Key : ....

(b)

Key : ....

(c)

Key : ....

(d)

Key : ....

(e)
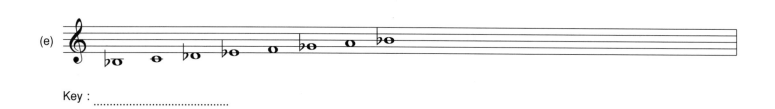

Key : ....

(f)
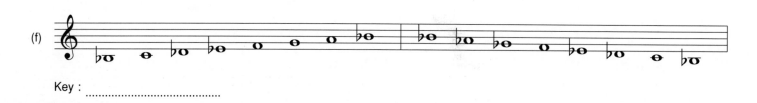

Key : ....

5. Insert the correct clef and accidentals to form the scales named.

(a)   B major

(b)   D♭ major

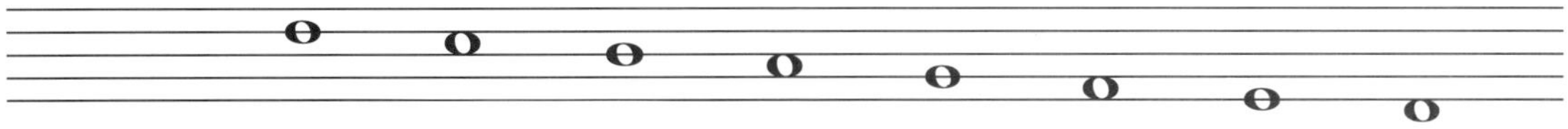

(c)   B♭ harmonic minor

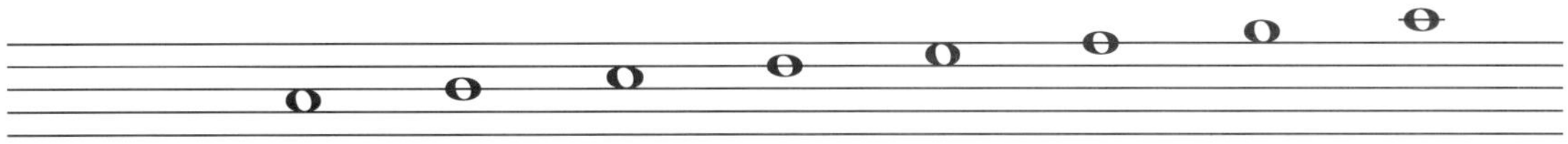

(d)   B major

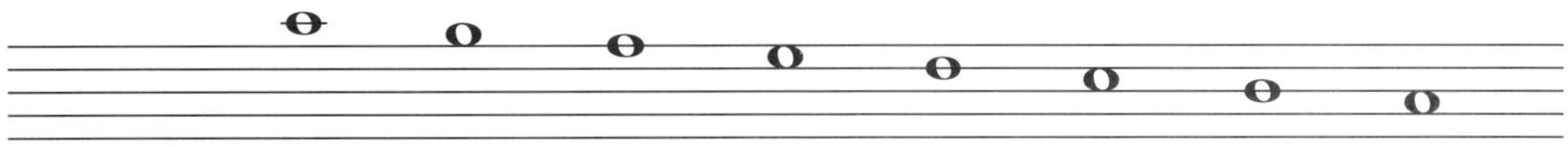

(e)   G♯ harmonic minor

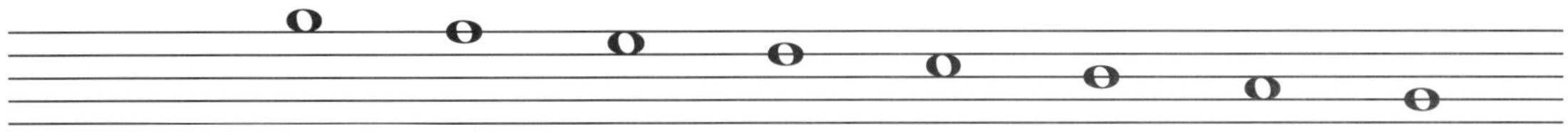

(f)   G♯ melodic minor

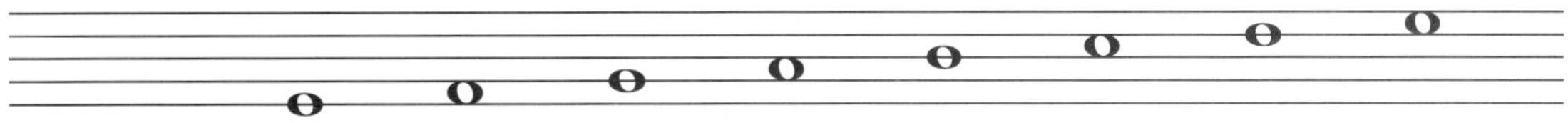

(g)   D♭ major

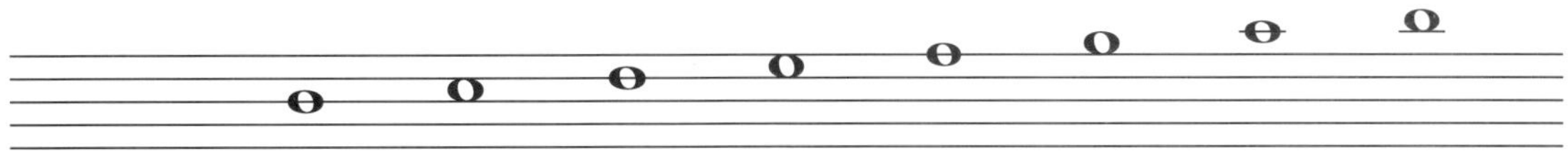

(h)   B♭ melodic minor

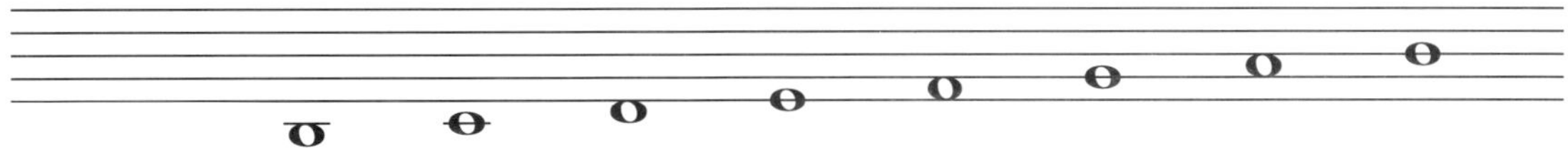

(i)   G♯ melodic minor

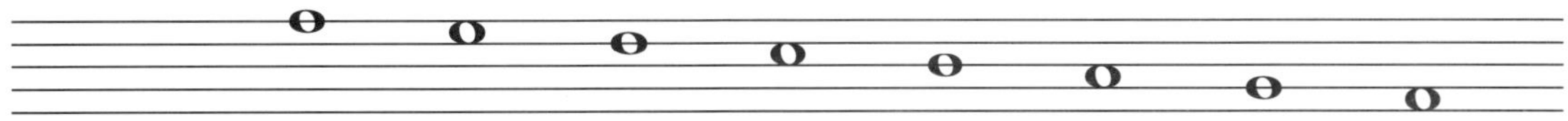

(j)   B♭ melodic minor

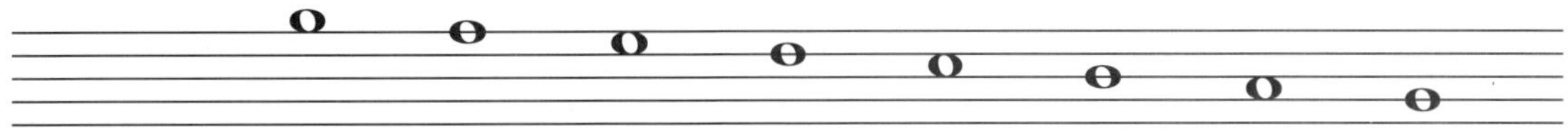

6. Name the key, then rewrite the passage using the correct key signature.

Technical names of notes of the scale

1	-	Tonic
2	-	Supertonic
3	-	Mediant
4	-	Subdominant
5	-	Dominant
6	-	Submediant
7	-	Leading-note

7. **Name the key then write the technical names of the notes.**

(a) *Scarlatti, Sonata in C minor L.352*

Key: ....

1. .... 2. .... 3. ....

4. .... 5. .... 6. ....

(b) *Mozart, Rondo 1*

Key: ....

1. .... 2. .... 3. ....

4. .... 5. .... 6. ....

(c) *Chopin, Valse*

Key: ....

1. .... 2. .... 3. ....

4. .... 5. .... 6. ....

(d) *Schubert, Who Is Sylvia?*

Key: ....

1. .... 2. .... 3. ....

4. .... 5. .... 6. ....

(e) *Haydn, Quartet in E♭ Op.76 No.6*

Key: ....

1. .... 2. .... 3. ....

4. .... 5. .... 6. ....

Grade 4

1. Add the correct clef and accidentals to make the scales named below.
Do not use key signatures. Complete the last bar with a rest or rests.

(a) C♯ harmonic minor

(b) F harmonic minor

(c) D melodic minor

(d) F melodic minor

2. Name each of the following notes. Then rewrite them in the bass clef at the same pitch.

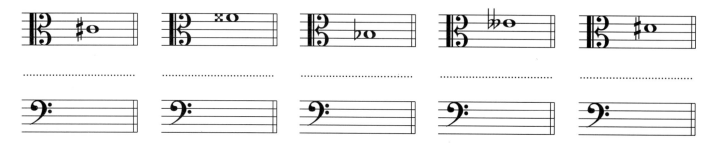

3. Add a time signature to each of the following. Also describe the time as *Simple* or *Compound*.

Duple

(a)

Time: ....

Triple

(b)

Time: ....

Quadruple

(c)

Time: ....

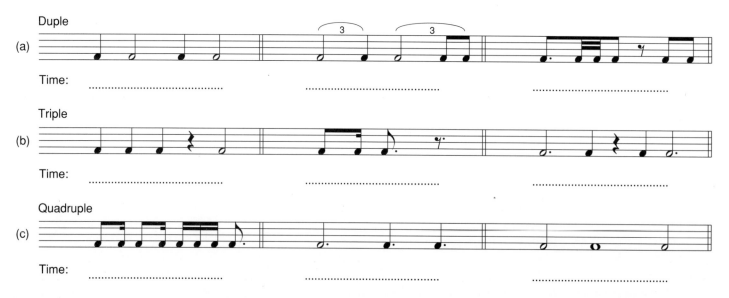

1. Compose four-bar rhythms beginning as follows.

(a)

(b)

(c)

(d)

(e)

(f)

(g)

(h)

(i)

(j)

2. Use each of the following in a four-bar rhythm but not necessarily at the beginning.

(a) a triplet in $\frac{3}{4}$

_____

(b) a duplet in $\frac{6}{8}$

_____

(c) a double dotted crotchet in $\frac{4}{4}$

_____

(d) 2 consecutive quaver rests in $\frac{6}{8}$

_____

(e) 25 notes in $\frac{3}{4}$

_____

(f) 20 notes in $\frac{4}{4}$

_____

In Grade 4, pupils are expected to know the 3 Primary Triads:

Tonic Triad, Subdominant Triad, Dominant Triad.

These triads are indicated by Roman Numerals: I, IV, V.

Below are some examples:

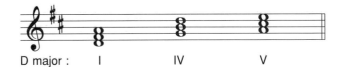

D major :   I   IV   V

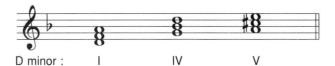

D minor :   I   IV   V

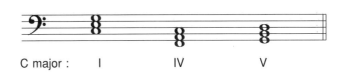

C major :   I   IV   V

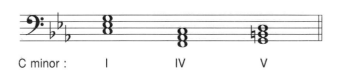

C minor :   I   IV   V

(Note: The V triad in a minor key consists of 5 7 2, so remember to raise the 7th note a semitone.)

1. **Write the key signature followed by the 3 Primary Triads. Identify the triads by writing I, IV, V below.**

(a)

A major   ....

(e)

C♯ minor   ....

(b)

E♭ major   ....

(f)

F minor   ....

(c)

D♭ major   ....

(g)

B♭ minor   ....

(d)

B major   ....

(h)

G♯ minor   ....

2. Identify the triads by writing I, IV or V below.

(a)

B minor   ....

(e)

F♯ minor   ....

(i)

D minor   ....

(m)

G minor   ....

(b)

E major   ....

(f)

G♯ minor   ....

(j)

A♭ major   ....

(n)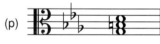

B♭ minor   ....

(c)

G major   ....

(g)

D major   ....

(k)

F major   ....

(o)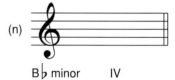

B♭ major   ....

(d)

A major   ....

(h)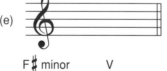

C♯ minor   ....

(l)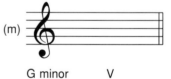

C major   ....

(p)

C minor   ....

3. Write the triads without key signatures but adding necessary accidentals.

(a)

B minor   I

(e)

F♯ minor   V

(i)

D minor   IV

(m)

G minor   V

(b)

E major   V

(f)

G♯ minor   V

(j)

A♭ major   I

(n)

B♭ minor   IV

(c)

G major   I

(g)

D major   V

(k)

F major   I

(o)

B♭ major   IV

(d)

A major   IV

(h)

C♯ minor   V

(l)

C major   IV

(p)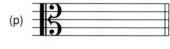

C minor   I

Pupils should be able to recognise chords made from the notes of the 3 Primary Triads.

In Grade 4, the chords are in "root position".

This means that the lowest note of the triad (the root) is at the bottom.

4. **Name the key, then identify the chords by writing I, IV or V below.**

(a)

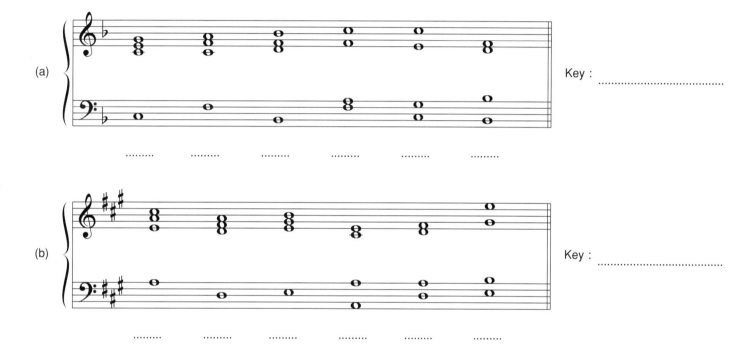

Key : ....

....

(b)

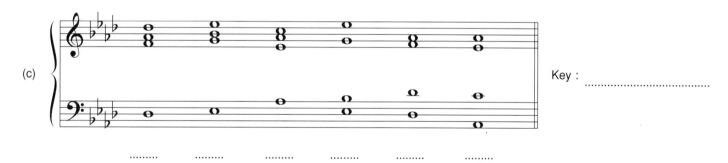

Key : ....

....

(c)

Key : ....

....

(d)

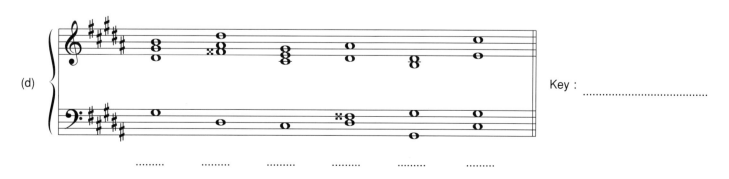

Key : ....

....

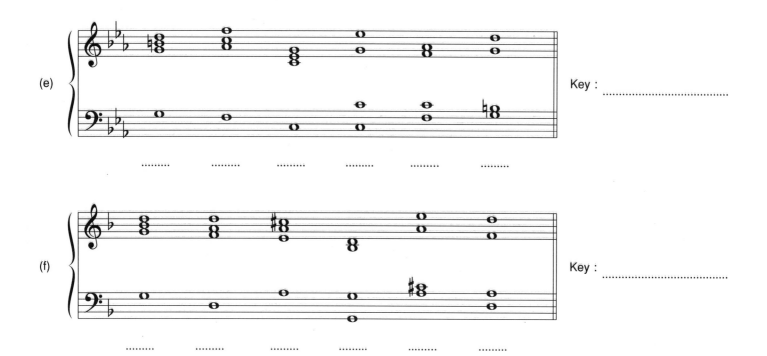

(e)

Key : ....

....

(f)

Key : ....

....

THIS CHART IS FOR REFERENCE

C	C	D	E	F	G	A	B	C	D
	1	2	3	4	5	6	7	1	2
D	D	E	F	G	A	B	C	D	E
	1	2	3	4	5	6	7	1	2
E	E	F	G	A	B	C	D	E	F
	1	2	3	4	5	6	7	1	2
F	F	G	A	B	C	D	E	F	G
	1	2	3	4	5	6	7	1	2
G	G	A	B	C	D	E	F	G	A
	1	2	3	4	5	6	7	1	2
A	A	B	C	D	E	F	G	A	B
	1	2	3	4	5	6	7	1	2
B	B	C	D	E	F	G	A	B	C
	1	2	3	4	5	6	7	1	2

Intervals

In Grade 1 - 3 intervals have been formed from the key-note only.
In Grade 4 intervals may be formed from any note of the scale.

Besides the major, minor and perfect intervals, augmented and diminished intervals are now added.

1. **MAJOR** interval becomes **AUGMENTED** when increased a semitone.
2. **MAJOR** interval becomes **MINOR** when decreased a semitone.
3. **MINOR** interval becomes **DIMINISHED** when decreased a semitone.
4. **PERFECT** interval becomes **AUGMENTED** when increased a semitone.
5. **PERFECT** interval becomes **DIMINISHED** when decreased a semitone.

When asked to name an interval, treat it at its simplest form and then build up to the required interval.

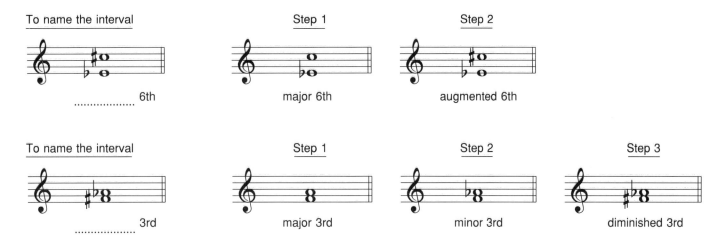

Strictly for checking only (to be omitted if found confusing)

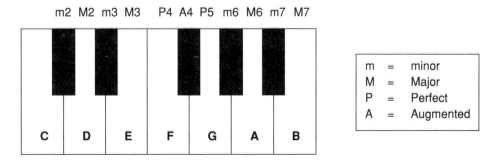

This is a fast method to check intervals. It applies to all keys
ie. after the tonic is minor 2nd, followed by major 2nd, minor 3rd, major 3rd, etc.
Note that Aug. 4th is also Dim. 5th;
minor 6th is also Aug. 5th;
minor 7th is also Aug. 6th; and so on.

1. Name the following intervals (Augmented or Diminished).

(a)

Name : ....

(b)

Name : ....

2. Name the following intervals.

(a)   (g)   (m)   (s)

Name : ....

(b)   (h)   (n)   (t)

Name : ....

(c)   (i)   (o)   (u)

Name : ....

(d)   (j)   (p)   (v)

Name : ....

(e)   (k)   (q)   (w)

Name : ....

(f)   (l)   (r)   (x)

Name : ....

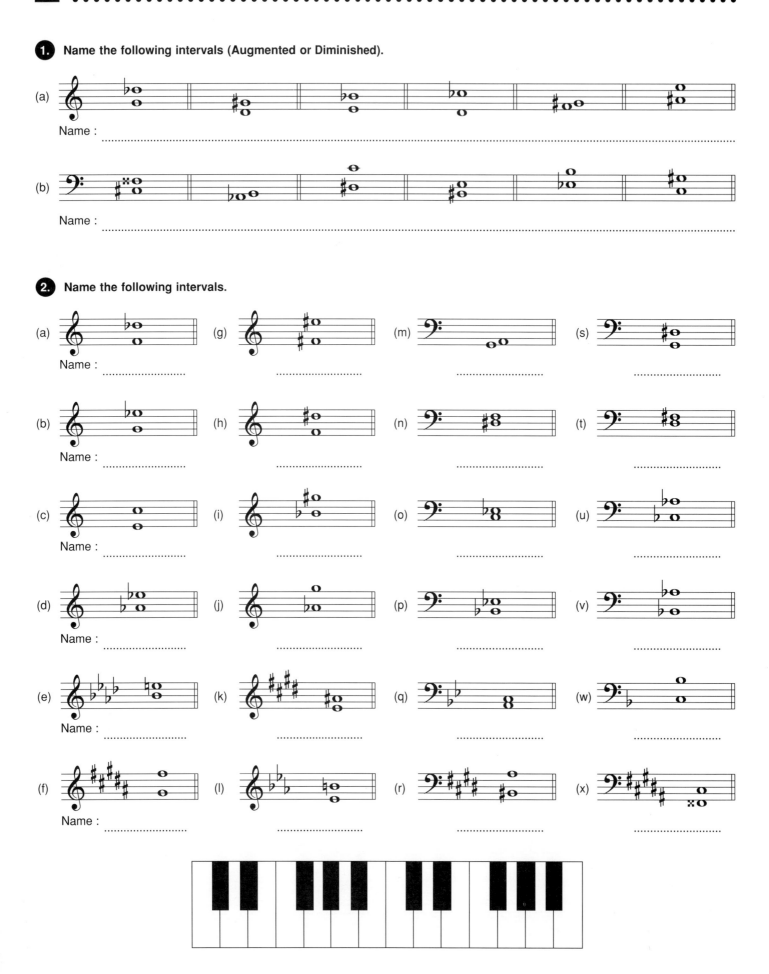

3. **Write the intervals required**

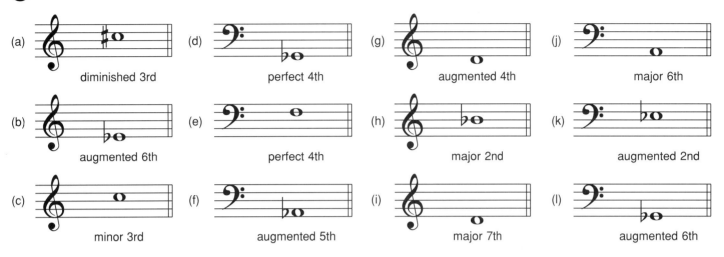

(a) diminished 3rd

(d) perfect 4th

(g) augmented 4th

(j) major 6th

(b) augmented 6th

(e) perfect 4th

(h) major 2nd

(k) augmented 2nd

(c) minor 3rd

(f) augmented 5th

(i) major 7th

(l) augmented 6th

4. **Name the intervals marked in square brackets ().**

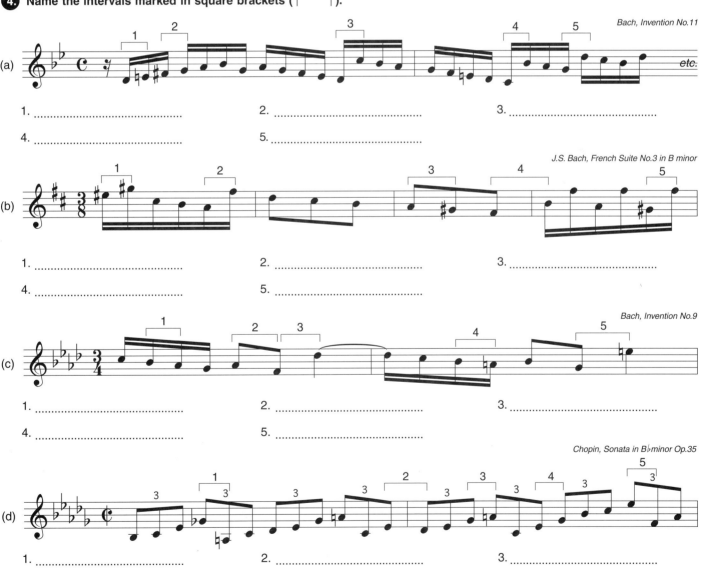

Bach, Invention No.11

(a)

1. ....
2. ....
3. ....
4. ....
5. ....

J.S. Bach, French Suite No.3 in B minor

(b)

1. ....
2. ....
3. ....
4. ....
5. ....

Bach, Invention No.9

(c)

1. ....
2. ....
3. ....
4. ....
5. ....

Chopin, Sonata in B♭ minor Op.35

(d)

1. ....
2. ....
3. ....
4. ....
5. ....

Writing a Rhythm to Given Words

In Grade 4, pupils may choose to write a rhythm to given words or to write a four-bar rhythm.

Writing a rhythm to fit given words

1. Read through the lines.
2. Indicate the accented (important) syllables with short lines as shown.
3. Write the words on the dotted lines.
4. Put bar-lines where accents occur.
5. Write the rhythm on the line above.

Remember to beam notes where necessary, even when at different syllables.

Example

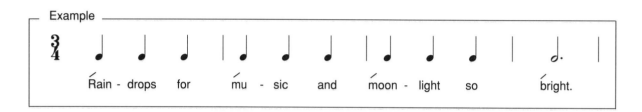

1. **Write a rhythm for each of the following.**
(Make sure each syllable is written under the note or notes to which it is to be sung.)

(a)

Cheer and clap, cheer and clap,
The runners are on the last lap;
Clap and cheer, clap and cheer,
For all the runners to hear.

(b)

And here beneath the blue, blue sky
Sat the King and I.

_____

....

_____

....

_____

....

_____

....

(c)

When the sky gets too dark, The seas too violent,
Remember the sweetness of yesterday.

_____

....

_____

....

_____

....

_____

....

(d)

A picnic we will go, A picnic we will go;
Hey ho a dally O, A picnic we will go.

_____

....

_____

....

_____

....

_____

....

(e)

Sitting by the window,
Watching swallows fly;
Makes me really wonder,
How high is the sky.

_____

....

_____

....

_____

....

_____

....

(f)

The wind doth blow today, my love,
And a few small drops of rain;
I never had but one true love,
In a cold grave she was lain.

_____

....

_____

....

_____

....

_____

....

Chromatic Scale

There are a variety of ways to write the chromatic scale. It should be written in whatever way seems convenient, using as few accidentals as possible and bearing in mind the key signature if there is one.

RULES

(a) 1 octave of chromatic scale consists of 13 notes.

(b) The same letter name must not be used more than twice in succession. (D♭ - D♮ - D♯ = wrong)

Below are 3 different ways of writing the chromatic scale beginning on E flat.
Always check your answer with the keyboard.

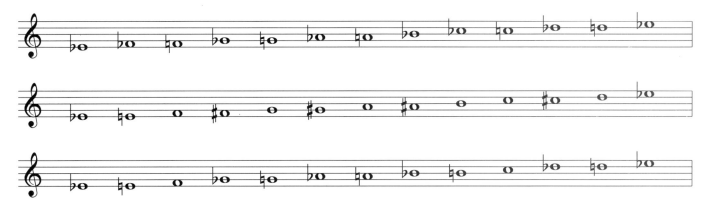

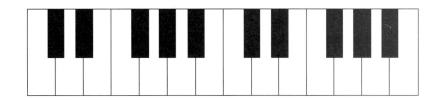

1. Insert accidentals to form chromatic scales.

(a)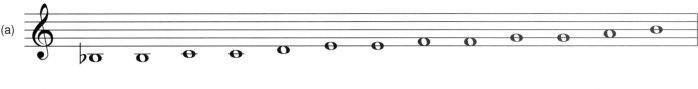

(b)

(c)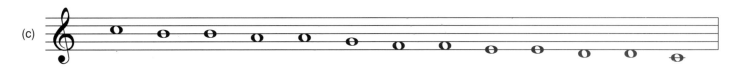

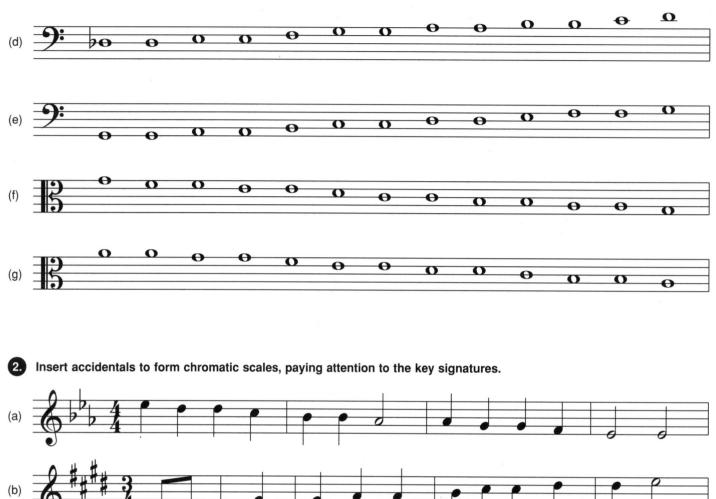

2. Insert accidentals to form chromatic scales, paying attention to the key signatures.

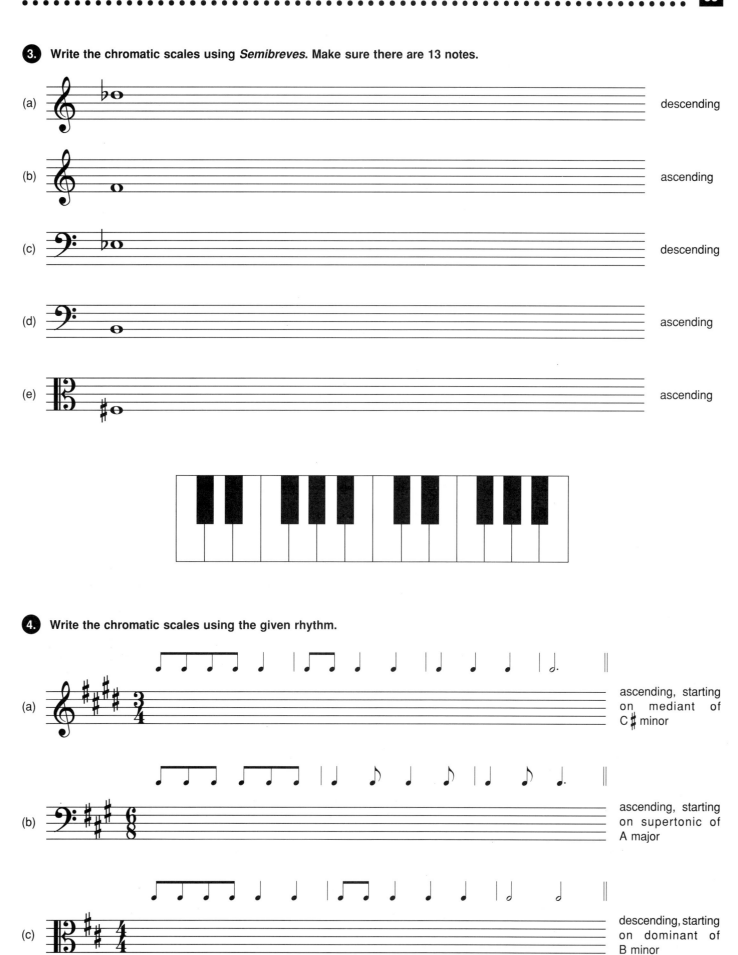

3. Write the chromatic scales using *Semibreves*. Make sure there are 13 notes.

(a)   descending

(b)   ascending

(c)   descending

(d)   ascending

(e)   ascending

4. Write the chromatic scales using the given rhythm.

(a)   ascending, starting on mediant of C♯ minor

(b)   ascending, starting on supertonic of A major

(c)   descending, starting on dominant of B minor

Grade 4

Revision 2

1. Describe fully each of these intervals.

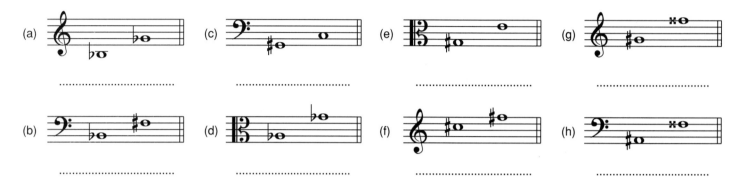

(a) ....

(c) ....

(e) ....

(g) ....

(b) ....

(d) ....

(f) ....

(h) ....

2. Write a note above each of the given notes to form the named intervals.

minor 7th   diminished 5th   major 6th   augmented 4th

3. Write a chromatic scale in *Semibreves*, descending one octave from the given note.

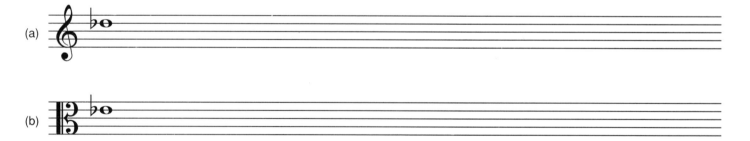

(a)

(b)

4. Write the named triads using accidentals. Do not use key signatures.

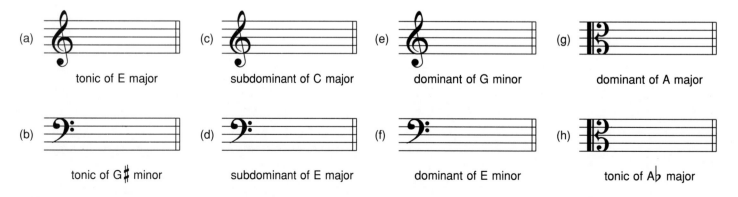

(a) tonic of E major

(c) subdominant of C major

(e) dominant of G minor

(g) dominant of A major

(b) tonic of G♯ minor

(d) subdominant of E major

(f) dominant of E minor

(h) tonic of A♭ major

5. Name each of the following notes (e.g. E double flat).

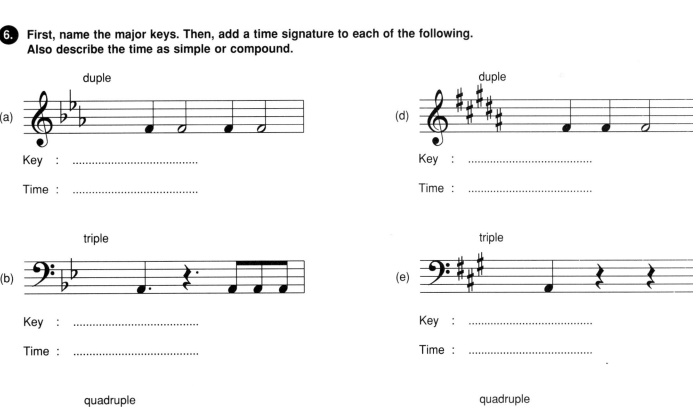

(a) ....

(b) ....

(c) ....

6. First, name the major keys. Then, add a time signature to each of the following.
Also describe the time as simple or compound.

(a) duple

Key : ....

Time : ....

(b) triple

Key : ....

Time : ....

(c) quadruple

Key : ....

Time : ....

(d) duple

Key : ....

Time : ....

(e) triple

Key : ....

Time : ....

(f) quadruple

Key : ....

Time : ....

7. Name each of the numbered chords as tonic, subdominant or dominant.

The key is A♭ major.

(a)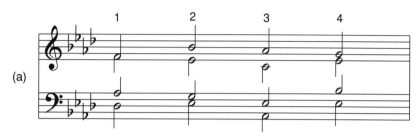

1. ....
2. ....
3. ....
4. ....

The key is D major.

(b)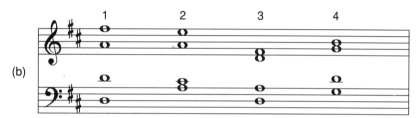

1. ....
2. ....
3. ....
4. ....

8. Add the correct time signature to each of the following. Also add a rest or rests to complete the last bars.

(a)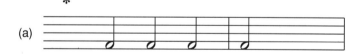

(f)

(b)

(g)

(c)

(h)

(d)

(i)

(e)

(j)

9. Add the correct clef and accidentals to make the scales named. Do not use a key signature.

(a) G♯ minor harmonic

(b) F♯ minor melodic

(c) F minor melodic

(d) D minor harmonic

(e) B♭ minor harmonic

10. Under each of the notes, write the number of the degree of the scale (2nd, 3rd, 4th, etc.) and also the technical name given to each (tonic, supertonic, etc.).

The key is E minor

(a)

Degree : ....

Technical Name : ....

The key is A major

(b)

Degree : ....

Technical Name : ....

Ornaments

In Grade 4, pupils are required to name the ornament signs.
Although pupils are not required to write out ornamented notes in full,
it is an advantage to know how the notes should be written.

The 6 ornaments that should be known are:

1. Acciaccatura
2. Appoggiatura
3. Mordent

4. Turn
5. Trill
6. Arpeggiation

The few examples below are acceptable, but there are varieties of
treatment and interpretation depending on the speed of the music.
For more details, refer to other materials on ornaments.

1. ACCIACCATURA (grace note / crushed note)

It is a small note (usually a quaver) with a stroke through its stem. It is played as quickly as possible.
It is theoretically timeless and is squeezed in before the principal note is heard.

2. APPOGGIATURA

(a) It is as important as the note on which it leans, and receives 1/2 the value of the principal note, divisible by 2.

(b) When placed before a dotted note divisible by 3, it gets 2/3 the value of the principal note.

3. MORDENT

(a) **Mordent** (upper mordent)
It consists of the main note, the note above and the main note again. An accidental affects the note above.

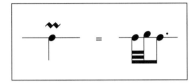 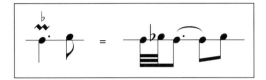

(b) **Inverted Mordent** (lower mordent)
It consists of the main note, the note below and the main note again. An accidental affects the note below.

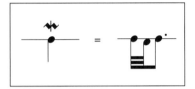 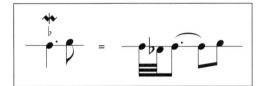

4. TURN

(a) **Turn** (upper turn)
It consists of 4 notes : the note above, the note itself, the note below, and the note itself.
An accidental above the sign affects the note above.
An accidental below the sign affects the note below.

(b) When the Turn is placed after a note, the principal note is held as long as possible, and the Turn is squeezed in quickly at the end.

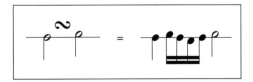 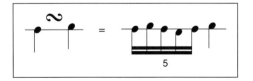

(c) **Inverted Turn** (lower turn)
It consists of 4 notes : the note below, the note itself, the note above, and the note itself.

5. TRILL (SHAKE)

(a) This is a rapid alternation of the principal note with the note above it. It usually ends with a Turn.

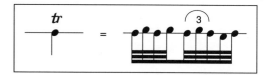

(b) When it occurs on a Repeated Note, begin with the upper note.
There will be no triplet in this case.

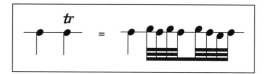

6. ARPEGGIATION

The notes are to be played one after the other as quickly as possible, starting from the bottom note.

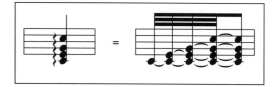

1. **Name the ornaments.**

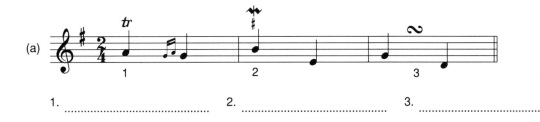

1. .... 2. .... 3. ....

1. .... 2. ....

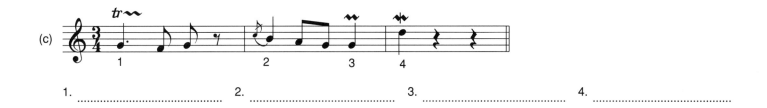

1. .... 2. .... 3. .... 4. ....

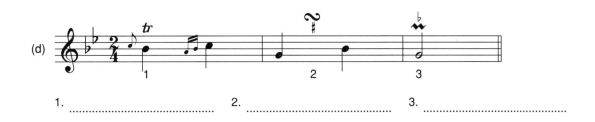

1. .... 2. .... 3. ....

2. **Write out the ornaments in the brackets.**

(a) acciaccatura (   )   (e) appoggiatura (   )

(b) mordent (   )   (f) arpeggiation (   )

(c) trill (   )   (g) inverted mordent (   )

(d) turn (   )   (h) lower turn (   )

3. Add the sign for a turn at the places marked ↑.

4. Write an acciaccatura before and a note higher than, each of the notes marked ↑.

5. Write the ornaments at the places marked ↑, or before the notes.

(a)

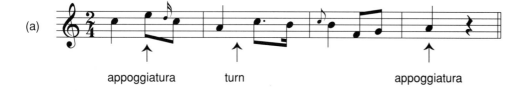

appoggiatura   turn   appoggiatura

(b)

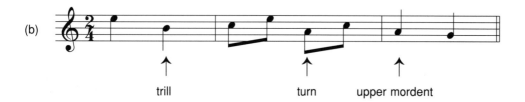

trill   turn   upper mordent

(c)

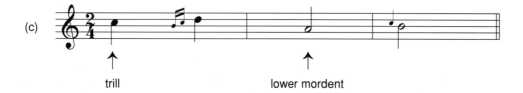

trill   lower mordent

(d)

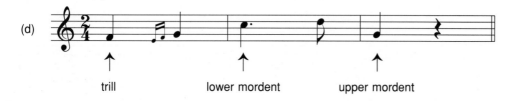

trill   lower mordent   upper mordent

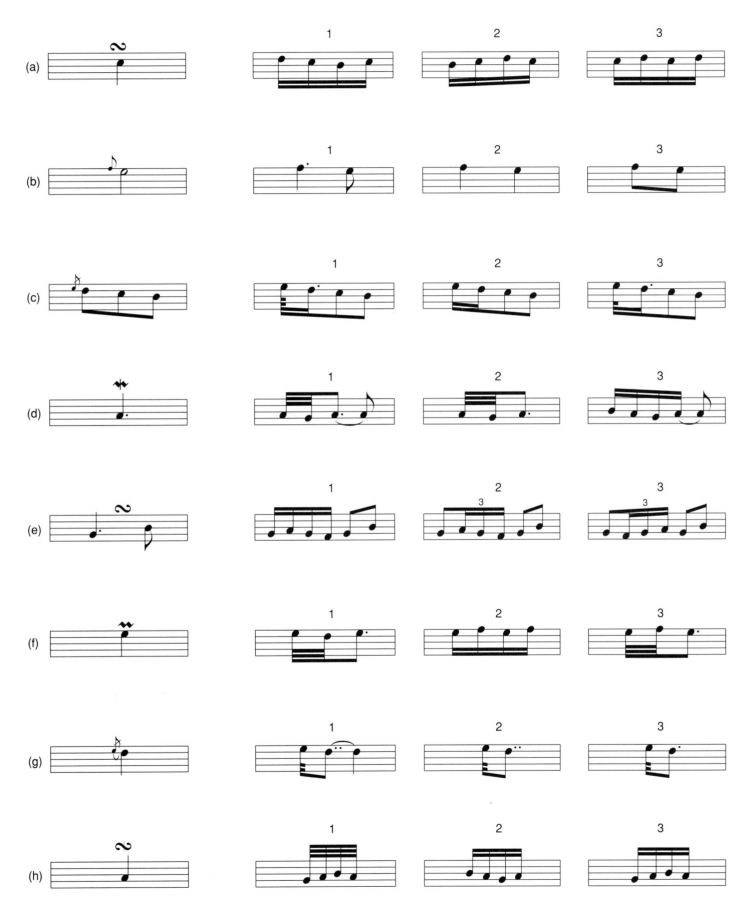

6. Circle which you think is the best way to play the ornamented notes. (1 ② 3)

In Grade 4, pupils may be asked about standard orchestral or keyboard instruments.
This chapter provides a rough idea of what you should know.
Please refer to other books for more information.

List of instruments beginning with highest in pitch.

STRING (Violin Family)

1. * Violin - smallest string instrument
2. * Viola
3. * Violoncello ('cello)
4.   Double Bass (Contra Bass)

WOODWIND

1.   Piccolo
2. * Flute
3. * Oboe
4.   Cor anglais (English horn)
5. * Clarinet (in B♭ and A)
6. * Bassoon

BRASS

1. * Trumpet
2. * Horn
3.   Cornet
4. * Trombone
5.   Bass trombone
6.   Tuba

(Instruments marked * are main orchestra instruments)

PERCUSSION INSTRUMENTS

Definite Pitch

1.   Glockenspiel (keyboard)
2.   Celesta   (keyboard)
3. * Kettledrum   (Timpani)
4.   Xylophone
5.   Dulcitone
6.   Tubular bells
7.   Marimba gong

Indefinite Pitch

1. * Drums - side (snare), bass
2. * Tambourine
3.   Triangle
4.   Castanets
5. * Cymbals
6.   Gong

COMBINATION OF INSTRUMENTS / VOICES

1. Piano Duet   - piano, violin
                     piano, cello
   Piano Trio   - piano, violin, 'cello
   Piano Quartet   - piano, violin, viola, 'cello
   Piano Quintet   - piano, 2 violins, 1 viola, 1 'cello

2. Vocal Quartet   - soprano, alto, tenor, bass (S.A.T.B.)
   Vocal Quintet   - 2 sopranos, contralto, tenor, bass

3. String Trio   - 1 violin, 1 viola, 1 'cello
   String Quartet - 2 violins, 1 viola, 1 'cello
   String Quintet - 2 violins, 2 viola, 1 'cello
                     2 violins, 1 viola, 2 'cello
                     2 violins, 1 viola, 1 'cello, 1 double bass
4. Clarinet Quintet - clarinet, string quartet

GROUP OF INSTRUMENTS BEGINNING WITH HIGHEST IN PITCH : STRING

NAME	CLEF	FEATURES	T / NT	TUNED	TUNED	COMPASS	MISCELLANEOUS
* Violin	𝄞	4 Strings, Bowing, Tremolo, Pizzicato, With / Without Mutes	NT	GDAE (5th)			Smallest string instrument
* Viola	𝄡a 𝄞		NT	CGDA (5th)		C clef / alto clef	Slightly larger than violin 5th lower than violin
* Violoncello ('Cello)	𝄢 𝄞 𝄡t		NT	CGDA (5th)			8th lower than viola
Double Bass	𝄢 𝄡t		NT	EADG (4th)			

The string family consists the largest number of players in an orchestra.
String Instruments can play 2, 3 or 4 notes simultaneously.
T = Transposing instrument
NT = Non-transposing instrument

𝄡a = alto clef   𝄡t = tenor clef

𝄢 / 𝄞 / 𝄡t = cello uses bass clef but sometimes treble or tenor clefs are used.

GROUP OF INSTRUMENTS BEGINNING WITH HIGHEST IN PITCH : WOODWIND

NAME	CLEF	FEATURES	SOUND	T / NT	MISCELLANEOUS
Piccolo	𝄞	Holes	8th Higher	NT	8th higher than flute
* Flute	𝄞	Holes	Bass Flute - 4th lower Concert Flute in D or C	T / NT	Modern flutes are made of metal Ordinary flutes are non-transposing instruments
* Oboe	𝄞	2 Reeds		NT	sounds the 'A' of the orchestra
Cor Anglais (English Horn)	𝄞	2 Reeds	5th lower	T	
* Clarinet	𝄞	1 Reed	B♭ - Tone lower A - Min 3rd lower	T	
* Bassoon	𝄢 𝄡t	2 Reeds			Lowest member of WW family in constant use
Double Bassoon	𝄢	2 Reeds	8th lower	NT	
Saxophone	Brass WW	1 Reed	Soprano in B♭ / Tenor in B♭ Bass in B♭ / Alto in E♭ Baritone in E♭ etc.	T	Also belong to Brass Group Consists of 8 instruments

Wind instruments can play only one note at a time.
Instruments which sound an octave higher or lower are usually considered non-transposing.
Reed   = a thin cane or metal which vibrates to produce a sound.
1 Reed = single reed
2 Reeds = double reed

GROUP OF INSTRUMENTS BEGINNING WITH HIGHEST IN PITCH : BRASS

NAME	CLEF	FEATURES	SOUND	T / NT	MISCELLANEOUS
* Trumpet	𝄞	3 Valves (Mutes)	Several keys B♭ - Tone lower A - Min 3rd lower	T	Soprano of brass family
* Horn (French Horn)	𝄞 𝄢	3 Valves (Mutes)	Horn in F - 5th lower	T	Full orchestra - 4 horns
Cornet	𝄞	3 Valves (Mutes)	Cornet in B♭ - Tone lower Cornet in A - Min 3rd lower	T	Resemble modern trumpet in fingering and compass
* Trombone	𝄢 𝄡t	Slide	Tenor trombone in B♭ and bass trombone in G - sound the same as written so non-transposing	NT	Tenor trombone - most important member of the trombone family
Tuba	𝄢	3 Valves	Several keys	NT	Lowest in brass family

Answer the following questions about instruments.

1. Name a keyboard instrument. ....

    What clefs does this instrument use ? ...., ...

2. Name two percussion keyboard instruments. ...., ...

3. Name two percussion instruments often found in an orchestra. ...., ...

4. Name the main instruments in each group.

    String - ...., ..., ...

    Brass - ...., ..., ...

    Woodwind - ...., ..., ..., ...

5. A piece of music is written in the alto clef. Which string instrument is it written for ? ....

6. A piece of music is written in the bass clef. Name the instruments that can play it.

    String - ....

    Woodwind - ....

    Brass - ....

7. Which is the smallest string instrument ? ....

8. Name the soprano of the following families.

   String - ....

   Brass - ....

9. Which is the lowest member of the woodwind family in constant use ? ....

10. Each string instrument consists of .... strings.

   They can be played with a .... or sometimes plucked, and this is called ....

11. Which family consists of the largest number of players in an orchestra ? ....

12. Name an instrument that uses:

   a slide - ....

   valves - ....

   mutes - ....

13. Name a double-reed instrument. ....

14. Which family of instruments does the flute belong to ? ....

15. A piece of music is written in the treble clef. Name the instruments that can play it.

   Keyboard - ....

   Woodwind - ....

   String - ....

16. Which family of instruments can play 2, 3 or 4 notes simultaneously ? ....

   Which family of instruments can play only one note at a time ? ....

17. Name a woodwind instrument that also belongs to the brass group. ....

18. Name the combination of voices of a vocal quartet.

   ...., ..., ..., ...

19. Name the combination of instruments for a string quartet.

   ...., ..., ..., ...

20. Name the combination of instruments for a clarinet quintet.

   ...., ..., ..., ..., ...

Italian terms - Grade 3

adagietto	-	rather slow (but faster than *adagio*)
ad libitum (ad lib.)	-	at pleasure (speed and manner of performance left to the performer)
agitato	-	agitated
alla breve	-	2 minim beats (¢ , $\frac{2}{2}$)
amore	-	love (*amoroso*: loving)
anima	-	soul, spirit (*con anima*: with feeling, spirited)
animato	-	animated, lively (*animando*: getting more lively)
ben	-	well
brio	-	vigour (*con brio*: with vigour, lively)
comodo	-	convenient (*tempo comodo*: at a convenient speed)
deciso	-	with determination
delicato	-	delicate
energico	-	energetic
forza	-	force
largamente	-	broadly
leggiero	-	light, delicate
marcato (marc.)	-	marked, accented
marziale	-	martial (in a military style)
mesto	-	sad
pesante	-	heavy
prima, primo	-	first
risoluto	-	bold, strong
ritmico	-	rhythmically
rubato, tempo rubato	-	robbed (with some freedom of time)
scherzando, scherzoso	-	playful, joking
seconda, secondo	-	second
semplice	-	simple, plain
sempre	-	always
stringendo	-	getting faster
subito	-	suddenly
tanto	-	so much
tranquillo	-	calm, tranquil
triste, tristamente	-	sad, sorrowful
volta	-	time (*prima volta*: first time)

String and Brass

con sordini	-	with mutes
senza sordini	-	without mutes

String

arco	-	play with the bow bowing marks: ⊓ down bow, V up bow
⌒	-	a slur means the notes are to be played in one stroke of the bow (up or down)
pizzicato	-	pluck the string
sul G	-	play on the G string
sul ponticello	-	play near the bridge

Piano

una corda	-	press the left pedal (literally '1 string')
tre corda	-	release the left pedal (literally '3 strings')
𝄅Ped. * p ⌐	-	press / release the right pedal
mano destra (m.d.)	-	right hand
mano sinistra (m.s.)	-	left hand
⦚	-	arpeggiation (spread the notes of the chord quickly, starting from the bottom note)

Italian Terms

affettuoso	-	tenderly		*morendo*	-	dying away
affrettando	-	hurrying		*niente*	-	nothing
amabile	-	amiable, pleasant		*nobilmente*	-	nobly
appassionato	-	with passion		*perdendosi*	-	dying away
calando	-	getting softer, dying away		*possibile*	-	possible
cantando	-	singing		*presto possibile*	-	as fast as possible
come	-	as, similar to		*quasi*	-	as if, resembling
come prima	-	as before		*sonoro*	-	resonant, with rich tone
come sopra	-	as above		*sopra*	-	above
facile	-	easy		*sotto*	-	below
fuoco	-	fire		*sotto voce*	-	in an undertone
giusto	-	proper, exact		*tempo giusto*	-	in strict time
l'istesso	-	the same		*veloce*	-	swift
l'istesso tempo	-	at the same speed		voce	-	voice

French Terms

à	-	to, at		*non*	-	not
animé	-	animated, lively		*peu*	-	little
assez	-	enough, sufficiently		*plus*	-	more
avec	-	with		*presser*	-	hurry
cédez	-	yield, relax the speed		*en pressant*	-	hurrying on
douce	-	sweet		*ralentir*	-	slow down
en dehors	-	prominent		*retenu*	-	held back
et	-	and		*en retenant*	-	holding back, slowing a little
légèrement	-	light		*sans*	-	without
lent	-	slow		*très*	-	very
mais	-	but		*un, une*	-	one
moins	-	less		*vif*	-	lively
modéré	-	at a moderate speed		*vite*	-	quick

1. **Give the meaning of the following**

adagio molto -

adagio un poco mosso -

alla marcia -

allegretto -

allegro con brio -

allegro con spirito -

allegro molto moderato -

andante tranquillo -

andantino -

anime -

cantando -

con anima -

grazioso -

largo e maestoso -

maestoso -

mesto -

moderato e dolce -

molto largamente -

morendo -

pesante -

più lento -

poco cresc. -

sempre più mosso -

tenuto -

vivace non troppo -

1. Look at the extract below, then answer the questions.

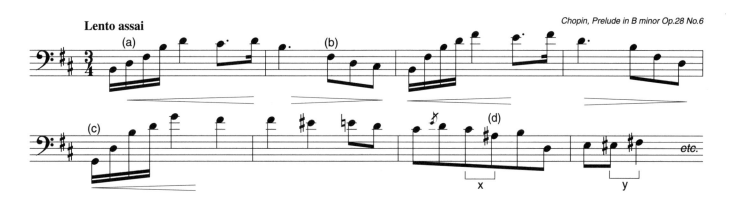

Lento assai

Chopin, Prelude in B minor Op.28 No.6

1. The key of this extract is B minor. Name the chord made by the first four notes in bar 1. .... chord.

2. Name the intervals marked X and Y.

    X = ...   Y = ...

3. Give the technical name of the notes marked a, b, c, d. (tonic, mediant, etc.)

    (a) = ...   (c) = ...

    (b) = ...   (d) = ...

4. What does lento assai mean? ....

5. Write the enharmonic equivalents (ie. a note which sounds the same but written differently) of the given notes.

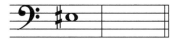   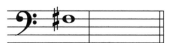

6. Name the ornament used in bar 7. ....

    How should it be played? ....

7. Name two standard orchestral instruments that can play this extract.

    woodwind = ...   string = ...

8. Rewrite bar 6 in compound time without changing the effect.

    $\frac{9}{8}$ ....

9. Rewrite the first two bars an octave higher using the treble clef.

10. Rewrite the first two bars at the same pitch in the alto clef.

2. Look at the extract below, then answer the questions.

Allegro moderato

Haydn, Sonata in C minor Hob XVI/20

1. Give the meaning of Allegro moderato. ....

2. Name one note which is chromatic to the key. ....

3. The ornament used in bar 2 has the same effect as ....

4. Name the following ornaments that appear in this extract.

   = ...   = ...   = ...

5. Give the technical names of the notes marked * .

   Bar 2 = ...   Bar 4 = ...

   Bar 3 = ...   Bar 6 = ...

6. Cross out two solo instruments that cannot play bars 1 and 5.

   flute   violin   trumpet

7. Name a standard orchestral string instrument which can play bars 6-8 an octave lower and name one of the clefs it uses.

   Instrument : ....   Clef : ....

8. This extract is made up of two main phrases. Mark the phrases in ⌐¬ above the stave.

9. Write out bar 1 an octave lower but in the alto clef.

10. Name one similarity and one difference between bars 1 and 5.

   similarity : ....

   difference : ....

3. Look at the extract below, then answer the questions.

Adagio molto

Beethoven, Sonata in C minor Op.10 No.1

1. Give the meaning of the following.

   Adagio molto - ....   *tr* - ....

   (slur) - ....   (bracket) - ....

   fp - ....

   (triplet) - ....

2. State the difference between bars 1-2 and bars 3-4.

   Bars 3-4 is ....

3. There are .... ♪s in a ♪..

4. This extract is in the key of A♭ major. Name a minor key which has the same key-signature.   .... minor.

5. Draw 2 circles round notes which are chromatic to A♭ major.

6. The notes in bar 5 are made up of notes of the .... chord.

   The notes in bar 6 are made up of notes of the .... chord.

7. Name a standard orchestral instrument which can play bars 1-5 sounding at this pitch, and the family to which it belongs.

   Instrument : ....   Family : ....

8. Name the lowest sounding instrument from the same family : ....

9. Draw a bracket ⌐‾‾⌐ over 3 notes next to each other that form part of a chromatic scale.

10. On the stave below, write the first 2 bars using the alto clef.

Grade 4

4. Look at the extract below, then answer the questions.

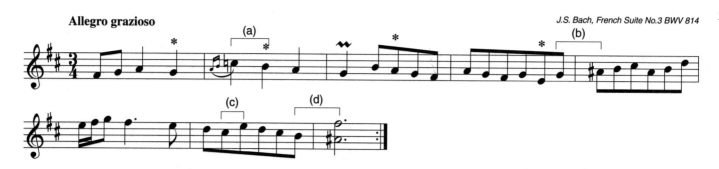

Allegro grazioso

J.S. Bach, French Suite No.3 BWV 814

1. Give the meaning of Allegro Grazioso. ....

2. The extract begins in the key of .... and modulates to .... from bar 5.

3. Give the technical name of the notes marked * . (eg. tonic, supertonic, etc.)

    Bar 1 : ....
    Bar 3 : ....

    Bar 2 : ....
    Bar 4 : ....

4. Write the enharmonic equivalents of the notes given.

     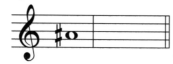 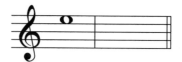

5. Name the intervals marked (a), (b), (c), (d).

    (a) - ....
    (c) - ....

    (b) - ....
    (d) - ....

6. Name the ornaments used in   Bar 2 : ....

    Bar 3 : ....

7. Cross out 3 orchestral instruments that cannot play bars 1-7 at the written pitch.

    violin   tuba   flue   bassoon   cello   trumpet

8. Name a chord which can be used to accompany the last bar. ....

9. Rewrite bars 1-2 in notes of half the value, using the new time-signature (exclude ornaments).

10. Rewrite bars 3-4 at the same pitch, using the alto clef.